BELLMAN VISITS SOUTH CAROLINA

Brenda Richards & Brantley Parrott

Library of Congress Control Number: 2008908341
ISBN 978-0-9820489-1-7

Published by Generation Press, LLC, Hopkins, South Carolina

Printed by RL Bryan, Columbia, South Carolina

Printed in the United States of America

A portion of the proceeds from the *Bellman Bear Series* will go to organizations that help children around the world. Please visit our website for more information about specific charities that receive aid because of your purchase.

www.bellmanbear.com

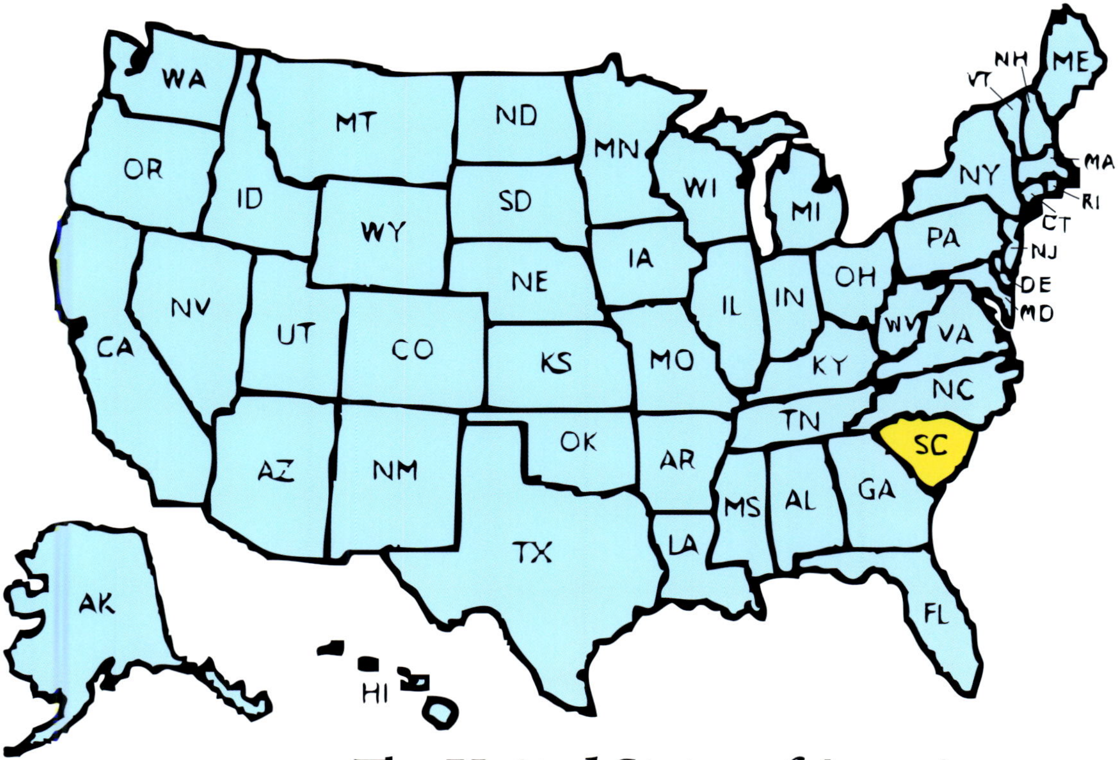

The United States of America

I can't wait to explore South Carolina!

HI! My name is
Bellman Bear,
and I love to travel.

I have enjoyed my adventures all over the world,
but my favorite place to visit is my home state,

South Carolina.

We are called the *Palmetto State*
because we are strong and flexible like palmetto trees.

Also, palmetto trees helped us during an important battle.

BELLMAN'S MAP OF SOUTH CAROLINA

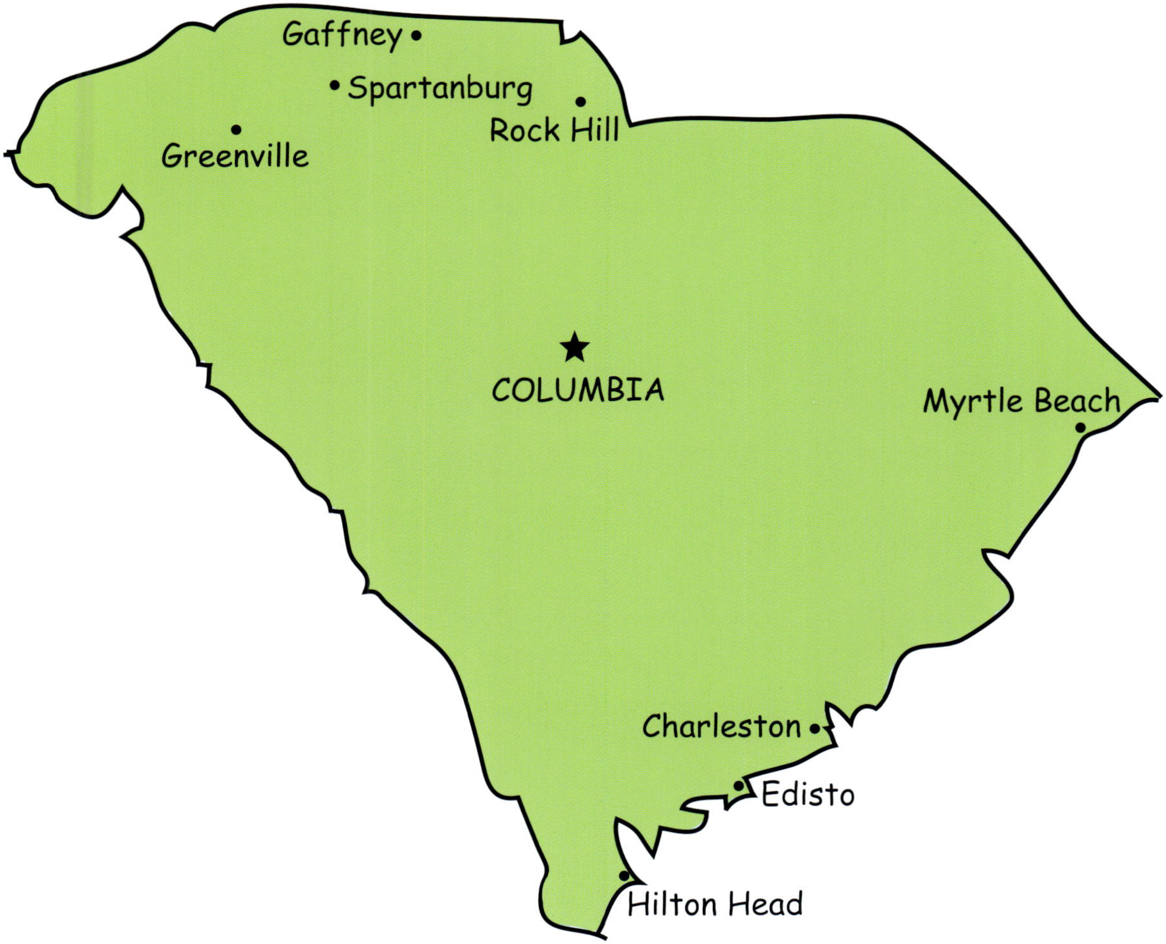

Our state flag is dark blue
with a white palmetto tree and a crescent moon on it.

Have you ever seen a crescent moon in the sky?
I like to go outside at night and look at the moon.

Sometimes it is a crescent moon,
sometimes it is a half moon,
sometimes it is a full moon,
and sometimes it is in between.

I wonder how the moon will look tonight...

Here are some fun facts about South Carolina!

State Capital: Columbia

State Animal: Whitetail Deer
State Bird: Carolina Wren
State Dog: Boykin Spaniel
State Fish: Striped Bass

State Fruit: Peach
State Flower: Yellow Jessamine
State Tree: Sabal Palmetto

We have already learned a lot about South Carolina.

Are you ready to discover all of the wonderful places here? We will begin our trip in the northern part of the state, which is sometimes called the Upstate or the Piedmont. Piedmont means "land at the foot of the mountains."

Greenville, Spartanburg, and Rock Hill are the largest cities in the Piedmont.

FALLS PARK IN GREENVILLE

South Carolina has
a lot of great state parks!
One of my favorites is
Table Rock State Park in the Upstate.

My dog, Hobbes, and I are going
to hike all the way to the top!

Would you like to go with us?

South Carolina
is famous
for its peaches.

Look at this huge
peach in Gaffney!

The town of Gaffney
loves peaches so much;
they even painted one
on their water tower.

Isn't it funny to see a
peach in the sky?

I like to eat peaches!

YUM!

Now we will leave
the Upstate
and drive
to the middle
of the state,
which is called
the Midlands.

Columbia is the capital
of South Carolina,
and it is located
in the Midlands.

The State House is an
important building
because the Governor
and other lawmakers
work there.

Can you find me at the
State House?

HERE I AM!

I am sitting on the George Washington statue.

Did you know that George Washington was the first President of the United States?

Hundreds of years ago,
before South Carolina became a state
and before the United States became a country,
Native Americans lived here.

Have you ever heard of an artifact?

An artifact is an object made a long time ago.

I often walk in fields with my grandfather to hunt
for artifacts made by the Native Americans.

After explorers discovered North America, families from England traveled in ships to the new land.

Sometimes they made friends with the Native Americans, and sometimes they fought with them.

Eventually, the English settlers decided that they wanted to stay, and that they did not want the King of England to tell them what to do anymore.

They wanted to form their own country.

They wanted to be free.

Their fight with England is called the

Revolutionary War.

Do you remember when I told you that palmetto trees helped us during an important battle?

Well, Fort Moultrie was originally built with palmetto logs.

When England attacked during the Revolutionary War, the soft palmetto logs absorbed the cannon balls.

Some cannon balls even bounced off of them!

We finally won our freedom from England and became the United States of America.

The United States started off with 13 states, and South Carolina was the 8th state to join.

Charleston was the first capital of South Carolina.

Charleston is located in the southern part of the state, which is also called the Lowcountry.

Weaving
sweet grass baskets
is a special
tradition
in South Carolina,
especially
in Charleston.

I think they are
beautiful!

YO HO HO!

Did you know that pirates
used to sail
off the coast of Charleston?

When they were caught,
they were thrown
into a dungeon!

CIVIL WAR

We have already
learned about
Fort Moultrie.

Now we will visit
another
important fort,
Fort Sumter.

The first shots
of the Civil War
were fired here.

The Civil War
was a sad time
in American history
when the
Northern states
fought against
the Southern states.

Finally the North won,
and we
became
one nation again.

Our last stop in the Lowcountry is the beach.

South Carolina borders the Atlantic Ocean.

Some of our wonderful beaches are Myrtle Beach, Edisto Beach, and Hilton Head.

Do you like the beach?

There are a lot
of animals at the beach.

Look! Dolphins are
swimming by!

I also like to watch
the herons
and the egrets
in the marsh.

Shhh!

Don't make any noise.

We don't want
to scare them away!

I had a great time exploring South Carolina. I can't wait to travel with you again soon.

I am already dreaming about our next adventure!

ABOUT THE AUTHORS

When they are not busy building sand castles with Bellman, this mother and daughter enjoy learning new things and taking care of their families.

They share a love of children's books and hope that you will enjoy Bellman's adventures along with them!

Brenda, an elementary school teacher in South Carolina for 29 years, often used teddy bears to teach important lessons in her classroom. Now Bellman helps her continue to teach children through his traveling adventures. Each book focuses on history, map skills, and interesting facts.

Brantley, a Business Administration graduate, believes that the world becomes a greater place when we take the time to walk in someone else's shoes. Bellman's books allow children to do just that by introducing them to places and cultures that are different from their own experience.

We are excited to introduce the Bellman Bear Series and hope that Bellman's books will be a valuable tool for you to use as you teach your children about the United States and the world.

Bellman and the authors are available for school visits. Please visit our website for scheduling details.

www.bellmanbear.com

Check out these other great books
from the **Bellman Bear Series**

Meet Bellman the Traveling Bear

Bellman Goes to France

Bellman Goes to Greece

More books will be available soon because
Bellman has already planned his next trip!

Bear Hugs!
Bellman